Sky B

PETER GIZZI is the author of eight collections of poetry, most recently, *Archeophonics* (Finalist for the 2016 National Book Award), *In Defense of Nothing*, and *Threshold Songs*. His honors include the Lavan Younger Poet Award from the Academy of American Poets, and fellowships in poetry from The Rex Foundation, The Howard Foundation, The Foundation for Contemporary Arts, and The John Simon Guggenheim Memorial Foundation. He has twice been the recipient of The Judith E. Wilson Visiting Fellowship in Poetry at the University of Cambridge. His editing projects have included *o·blēk: a journal of language arts*, *The Exact Change Yearbook*, *The House That Jack Built: The Collected Lectures of Jack Spicer*, and, with Kevin Killian, *My Vocabulary Did This to Me: The Collected Poetry of Jack Spicer*. He is on the faculty at the University of Massachusetts, Amherst.

PETER GIZZI

Sky Burial

New & Selected Poems

C A R C A N E T

ACKNOWLEDGEMENTS

Poems in the new section have appeared in: *The Cambridge Literary Review*, *The Chicago Review*, *Conjunctions*, *The Forward Book of Poetry*, *Granta*, *Harper's*, *Hyperallergic*, *jubilat*, *Mote*, *New York Review of Books*, *Paris Review*, *The Poetry Review*, and *The World Speaking Back*.

This is the second printing

First published in Great Britain in 2020 by
Carcanet Press Ltd
Alliance House, 30 Cross Street
Manchester M2 7AQ
www.carcanet.co.uk

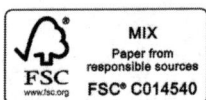

MIX
Paper from
responsible sources
FSC
www.fsc.org   FSC® C014540

A CfP catalogue record for this book is available from the British Library

ISBN 978 1 78410 822 9

The publisher acknowledges financial assistance from Arts Council England

Supported using public funding by
ARTS COUNCIL
ENGLAND

Typeset in England by XL Publishing Services, Exmouth
Printed and bound in England by SRP Ltd, Exeter

Contents

from THE OUTERNATIONALE (2008)

from THRESHOLD SONGS (2011)

from ARCHEOPHONICS (2016)

Speech Acts for a Dying World

A field sparrow
is at my window,
tapping at its reflection,
a tired
antique god
trying to communicate

it's getting to me

as I set out to sing
the nimbus of flora
under a partly mottled sky

as I look at the end
and sing so what,
sing live now,
thinking why not

I'm listening and
receiving now
and it feeds me,
I'm always hungry

when the beautiful
is too much to carry
inside my winter

when my library is full of loss
full of wonder

when the polis is breaking
and casts a shadow
over all of me,
thinking of it

when the shadows fall
in ripples, when
the medium I work in
is deathless and
I'm living inside
one great example
of stubbornness

as my head is stoved in
by a glance, as the day's
silver-tipped buds sway in union,
waving to the corporate sky

when I said work
and meant lyric

when I thought I was done
with the poem as a vehicle
to understand violence

I thought I was done
with the high-toned
shitty world

done with the voice and
its constituent pap

call down the inherited
phenomenal world
when it's raining in the book,
lost to the world
in an abundance of world

like listening to a violin
when the figure isn't native
but the emotion is

when everything is snow
and what lies ahead
is a mesmer's twirling locket

I thought I was done
with the marvel
of ephemeral shadow play,
the great design and all that

I thought I was done
with time, its theatricality,
glamour, and guff

gusting cloud, I see you,
I become you
in my solitary thinging,
here in partial light

when I said voice,
I meant the whole unholy grain of it,
it felt like paradise

meaning rises and sets,
now a hunter overhead
now a bear at the pole
and the sound of names

the parade of names

That I Saw the Light on Nonotuck Avenue

That every musical note is a flame, native in its own tongue.

That between bread and ash there is fire.

That the day swells and crests.

That I found myself born into it with sirens and trucks going by out here in a poem.

That there are other things that go into poems like the pigeon, cobalt, dirty windows, sun.

That I have seen skin in marble, eye in stone.

That the information I carry is mostly bacterial.

That I am a host.

That the ghost of the text is unknown.

That I live near an Air Force base and the sound in the sky is death.

That sound like old poetry can kill us.

That there are small things in the poem: paper clips, gauze, tater tots, and knives.

That there can also be emptiness fanning out into breakfast rolls, macadam, stars.

That I am hungry.

That I seek knowledge of the ancient sycamore that also lives in the valley where I live.

That I call to it.

That there are airships overhead.

That I live alone in my head out here in a poem near a magical tree.

That I saw the light on Nonotuck Avenue and heard the cry of a dove recede into a rustle.

That its cry was quiet light falling into a coffin.

That it altered me.

That today the river is a camera obscura, bending trees.

That I sing this of metallic shimmer, sing the sky, the song, all of it and wonder if I am dying would you come back for me?

Every Day I Want to Fly My Kite

Give the world
to the world,
time to the flood,
give ash to gardens
and grain to trees.
I am not cowed
by the superlative
nature in trees.
I am lifted
and see petals opening.

Give the freckled ground
to sun,
give sepulcher
to sky,
to song.
I am not one
to disregard thrush,
diminish sparrow.

Give the arrow
to lovers,
night to lavender,
lavender to sleep,
to wing
to want
to wound
to wonder
the night's watch,
the optical dawn.

Give water to stone,
stone to echo.
In the mosaic
the dove's wings

are made of bits
and stone.
The world is like this.

If I saw it
I felt it.
If I felt it
I learned from it.
And when the moon
opens the horizon,
that's Tuesday gone.

The moon
the silk
the corn
the rail.
I felt this and
it stuck to me
one midnight.
I was mewling.

I was alive with fancy
and silk and stuff.
I was stuffing for a chair,
a doll.
I was blinking
and crying and.

Now the word
falling.
Now other rains.
Now organics
cyclones and seeds.
The deadly swoon
in strength and
with color
and the sound
of crows and

their platinum sheen
feeding the sky.
Flames and greatness
towing the names.

Give home
to the horizon,
horizon to mystery,
mercy, meaning.
I thought I
might try to
head out
the door.
The door.
It doesn't
matter.
I go as long
as I go and if
you're there
to sparrow.
Sparrow.

Now It's Dark

Not the easiest day I'm having, clouds banking
and I dropped my signal.
I was trying to find my shoes and thought
I am overpowered by the gigantism
        of commercial governing.
As I looked for my shoes this morning
the thought was where am I going?
There isn't a place I can walk out from
        under this chemical sky.
So I thought I would write a poem.
I thought I would try and make art.
But the chemicals seep into everything.
Reader, if I could I would bring back for you
        a sun made in crayon.
A sun unformed in the paper sky.
I wonder the paper that made me.
Being human I know that paper makes my mind.
Strange pulp reminding me I am far away.
When my brother could no longer speak
        I said Tommy I got this
even if I don't want this, I'll sing for you.
When my brother had no voice there was only the couch
        and a wooden floor
the ceiling and the TV with nothing blaring.
When my brother lost his voice I lost my childhood
lost the sun over sand in some place I can't remember
        in Rhode Island summer.
So far from myself in a body I can't remember.
To no longer remember my body as a child.
To no longer remember today all that was.
Van Gogh was tormented by the sun and why not.
A constant blade-searing light that kills and cures.
I am not comforted by the cold stability
        of universal laws
though one day I will die and think, that's ok.

At least I'm writing and it makes a party in the dark.
A zombie feature that connects me to the undying.
I read every moment is an opportunity for grace
and think every moment is a possibility of art.
I tie my shoes and now I am standing alone
        in some inky light.
Yesterday I passed a Budget Motel next to
        the Peoples Bank.
If there's some connection it's lost on me.
My heart lost on me.
Weather like thought dissolves into static
a wiggy keepsake like nesting dolls of my
        spiritual blank.
Sky opening into blank.
I thought grief is a form of grace.
Then someone said the thing about money
        is that it's money.
I live on the edge of an expanding circumference
alone in some inky light.
Now rain turns the world to constant applause.
The day is uncoupled.
All there is is thunder as the house decays
        into a sound like me.
Freezing rain with silver seems to be speaking
and isn't asking me anything.
Just doing its thing in the gray morning.
I was down with materialism but
        wanted mystery.
I've asked myself a lot of questions like
        why the day's cascade
swiping left for life, right for lose.
All of it a dumb show.
All of me invested in poetry and the
        arrogance of this.
Wanting to transpose loneliness.
Why not take on the next life
        with its silence.
On my desk there are small plastic creatures.

The light on them is unrealistic.
It uncouples me.
Or the sight of serious windows opening out
    onto serious lawns.
This must be a government building.
This must be the anodyne room of
    a hospital beeping.
Every pronouncement on the feed, alien.
I'm in this corridor wandering a mind.
But the day is past caring.
The rhythmus is blooming at the beginning
    of the way back when.
I am sick with tradition and its weak signaling.
Sparkling eclogues drift and contribute
    little to the cause.
I am an incident trapped in thick description.
Just google it.
Dust jacket shows some rubbing,
    near fine in cloth.

Sunshine

Of what. Was wing.
Was bright all afternoon.

Was nothing
more than
collapsing into
the crisp March
late-winter air.

This sheaf of light.
It doesn't help.

Nowhere to tune
my voice, waiting.
My mental furniture
breaking.

I have blood
in my veins
and we go on
together trying
to decode
the swath of evil
across our sun-
sovereign bodies.

All I want
is the word
to reveal the day.

Want to understand
the this in that,
want this, got that
and ran with it.

Also the stanzas
against the capital
reeling from might.

Got to be with
the peoples who
said no, and
then said, yes.

The art of
the collective
as it collapses
into a poem.

Sometimes there
is a poem
and says my life.

Says what. Says wing.

Some Joy for Morning

Now the connection with spring has dissolved.

Now that hysteria is blooming.

Says every day I want to fly my kite.

Says what's a grammar when you is no longer you.

My world is hydrogen burning in space and in the fullness of etc.

I have read the news and learned nothing.

I try to understand the whooshing overhead.

But for a little light now.

I didn't realise the tree was weeping.

How was I to know I am not alone.

Wild light.

From This End of Sadness

A particular blur
attended my mind
from end to end.

These feelings
of futurelessness.

To free fall into it.

It feels like winter,
the light overcast
and the day lit up
from within.

To find a line in it.

I found a world
torched into renewal,
blackened stalks
pointing skyward.

I took fortification
from goneness.
At this end
the notation is green.

No stopping music
entering air
and tearing air,
the songs
were old songs.

They came
with the wren
and the robin.

Also the crow
so dear to reality
and elegy
and traffic,
its essential din.
The synesthesia
of the din.

From this end
of sadness
I identified
the voice as dead,
it was companionable.
I identified sky
turning topaz.

I did not
understand shadows,
did not understand
luminosity.

I did not understand
the code that held
me to the world.

From this end
glistening leaves,
cool air.

Wandering out into it,
wondering through it,
the day crumbles to dust
inside a blue dahlia.

I am that dust and dahlia.

I am coeval
with the rotting trunk
and the pine needles
regenerating soil.

I am happiest
with the forest floor,
branches listing
under a porcelain sky.

I'm into that medieval
light glancing
through leaves.
The tree's arches
are a great
kingdom now.

From this end
of sadness
there's nothing
out there I want
and wonder
if there's anything
in here I need?

I'm into the way
the technology of an I
is filled with the dead.

I'm heavy with light
when the old sun
is speaking,
when I'm not sure
the day is real.

When it's hard
to be in and of it,
to be here with it
and under it.

From this end of sadness
shapes come,
all the boldest shadows.

From this end animals,
the oldest eyes,
the *cri de Coeur*,
afternoons hung
with seeping light.

Poor sun,
waiting to die.
Poor sun
solo in space,
fueling
our heads,
a tiny sun
in the mind.

Right now,
a particle
decays
on the lawn.

From this end
gravity decays
in the mind.

To never forget
the corners
and dust bunnies
of the laughing sun.

But if the song
weren't a bright star
hanging in
the firmament
then what
can be said
for burning embers
in the fire.

I see you turning
and bending there
in the cold dream
of the past
braiding
with the now
of blur.

Blur with me
when I am sick
of dying,
fearful of failing
the song I love.

Be with me
whenever I sit
wasting days.

Comfort the hours.

Sky Burial

The robin that lives in my yard
also lives in me. This is the interior,
while the state unwinds across
a vast expanse splitting the sky.
It is all of it and more;
these things were passages
of the light-born afternoon
cascading then expanding
like a flange around the day.
Yes, the day, staccato
in its azure and gold banner;
then one learns, as one learns
from twilight, how to look
through here, and not here, grinning.
The wisteria out my window
is waving, up, down, up,
it's so far away though, outside.
I'm in here where the word is opening.
There are distances, the whole
tonal range blooming,
clarity of attenuated looking,
a payload delivering meaningful dust.
It's a good day to die.

Sunday's Empire

The roofs speak
as light over
the scaped silence.

A cacophony
of shapes
kicks off into sky.

People live here
in the quiet
a day undresses.

Tones shaking out.

Now It's Dark

No one gave me a greater thing
than their time.
But the old song,
worn from use,
is with me again.
So much of it
behind me now.
In front of me a slow season,
when a face passes
into a name.
Last night the moon was lolling
9 degrees over the horizon
but I didn't know.
I was in a fever dream
downloading ravens into my skull.
An unkindness of them.
This is called what it's like
to sleep alone for years.
It means all these years to remain
untouched wrote the poem.
I use my mouth to say goodbye,
fever dream, raven, skull.
To say like a flower, little dust.
To say what of it.
The world is close today
and elegy is my tonic.
I recast language in hope
of recovering the red oak
my neighbors felled.
It lived over a hundred years, glowing.
Now, neither music or rhyme,
just night, tin, and sky.

The Present Is Constant Elegy

Those years when I was alive, I lived the era of the fast car.

There were silhouettes in gold and royal blue, a half-light in tire marks across a field – Times when the hollyhocks spoke.

There were weeds in a hopescape as in a painted backdrop there is also a face.

And then I found myself when the poem wanted me in pain writing this.

The sky was always there but useless – And what of the blue phlox, onstage and morphing.

Chance blossoms so quickly, it's a wonder we recognize anything, wanting one love to walk out of the ground.

Passion comes from a difficult world – I'm sick of twilight, when the light is crushed, time unravels its string.

Along the way I discovered a voice, a sun-stroked path choked with old light, a ray already blown.

Look at the world, its veil.

Periplum

Put your map right with the world

The person who knows where
has made an accurate study

of here

As to know
implies a different reading

Somewhere

faith enters
and must be pinned and sighted

A church tower is good for reference
but losing ground

Still

satellites orbiting the earth
track a true arc

but perhaps too grand
for everyday distances

And never mind about the bewilderment

'I'm at sea'

Blue Peter

after Jasper Johns

To describe a logic of sight
pull the surface onto target and
arrive at zero aperture. Then
fluctuate to a face, reproduced
in serial format, superimposed
upon marginal pedestrians,
traversing a polarity of earth.

The axis here is askew, perhaps
unsettling, the way physical
equilibrium slides into multiple
perspective. This place where
sight informs the eye as gate
to phenomenon, a bridge to
impulse the imaginary. Simply

she was feeding bread to pigeons
in the park. So begin this sentence
with rain and square the surrounding
flat with common traffic. I
move through, to get here. If you
want me, you will find me in
the garden of vestiges, next to

the sweet water cistern. Where
the old port remains, a water
mark on granite, abutted with
grass and a stone path leading
to other places that for the moment
I am not interested in, as I take
serious your claim to provoke you.

And I will follow your instructions,
however silly, however sublime, until
you have found me, indistinguishable
from what you call, your self.
The way I wear you about my
mouth, as a crease, deepening
every time I smile to look at you.

Look at me. I'm serious, I must
find the way, to say, we have arrived.
For it is you who instruct me in
the laws of perspective, these many
converging lines, drawn to perception.
So that I have become only a star or
an asterisk or a compass rose. Signifying

location, this possibility of place. True.
It's been said that the burial of the dead
is the beginning of culture, as we know,
no other. And I remain raw.
Vapor digit tapping at my wrist,
the talon, the dorsal fin and the panther
claw. The value of negative space

and the rationale of talisman does
not parse, will not parry from this
dearth. As emotions surround the edge
of the planet adjusted to actual people we meet.
What could the difference of this construction
intend in a world of moments, merely
fragments provided to express conversation

or random noise signaling grey space,
to be inserted within an imported structure?
Birds migrate over cityscape and arrive
in my backyard to a mutiny of peaceful
dawn. Then a description of equality
is scored, as a rhetorical flourish is installed
for testimony. I flag. I stammer.

A banner to the burden that all things
that are, must not be, in me. Only,
will you not smile when I wave?

Poem for John Wieners

I am not a poet
because I live in the actual world
where fear divides light
I have no protection against
the real evils and money
which is the world
where most lives are spent

I am not a poet
because I cannot sing about
lost kingdoms of righteousness
instead I see a woman in a blue parka
crying on the street today
without hope from despair

I am not a poet
for there is nothing I can say
in smart turns to deflect
oncoming blows of every day's
inexistence that creeps into
the contemporary horizon

I am not a poet
but a witness to bear the empty
space that becomes our hearts
if left to loiter or linger
without a life to share

I've seen sorrow on joy street
and heard the blur of the hurdy-gurdy
and I too know what evening means
but this is not real – poetry is
and from this have I partaken
as my eyes grow into the evolved dark

Toy

You resist an ocean evaporating outside your head
You resist rain discovered outside small rooms

You resist daybreak invisible from grief
And the hollow inside is the shape of a flower

So the mouse has a purpose within its tiny office
And the butterfly isn't alive as a symbol ever

So that the smile independent from a person
And those glad tidings becoming empty

Look away from the joy of restorative morning
Easily opening to complete the long night

You are done in by sunrise and rightfully so
And those renewed theatrics of the skyline

Undo the hygiene of the visible body
Unlike a dove closing its wings at dawn

Go with a simple song, unbind yourself
Making sure to hide your giddy surface

Speck

Single the sky, pulled taut above earth
single the sky, above water. Bound
to bark and leaves. You are solo.

Blended into paint and forced into color
the song of a man in his bed at dusk
the sparrows lighting outside his window.

Ledger Domain

A morning's silver announces sky
Speech bent the tree into a new posture

My smile is becoming different from you.

– becoming – and you crave an earlier affection
Where was the silver becoming from?

Who forgets that we dream – who forgets we dream

The dark is near! That loss was dark; there that's darker!

A page, we become

*   *   *

You read the page
– you read this page

Once upon a once there was a once
and that once evaporated into air
it was said it once was all over the sky
then once came back and died

You understood what I saw
You understood everything

– close the door now

It knows where to be
Here, can you explain?

A light bulb replaced the silver

*   *   *

The page is silvery – almost as silver
– announced a child –

When it went to the town
– it had changed

When it became the town
– it changed its shape

Afterword said it didn't have its own way
It didn't have a once in its life –

a once and for all

It took a wife …

The end, the ending

*   *   *

Children ran from the tree
Silver poured from the sky

– in the garden birds bathed –
bathing in the garden birds sang

It was dizzy in the air and rosy on the wind

Once once came along and spoke to the bride

It thought the wood enchanted
Afterword said it was empty

Afterword came too and spoke to the groom

It thought the world was wide
Afterword said it was narrow

* * *

Syntax bent the child
– playing on the page

Speech – be quiet!

To see you reflected in the smudged window now.
Night reminds one of fingerprints –

unlike a face
– in its orbit

Tips of hair sweep by like fronds
– 'just like fronds!' – you exclaim

– show me the fronds if you please

* * *

Becoming a tree
– the children…

Becoming a page
– the birds in unison

From here to the nervous system – A body sang
Suspended above the page

Above the total mass of trees
Willows bend to console the child

From here to …

– a lovely thing –

Becoming a tree

* * *

Let us return to speech –

Silver morning – bent to break
– syntax

Up there on a stage
Children carry silver leaves

– carry birds on their heads

You fasten me with your songs
The Fables say –

where a page is a page
and a tree tree

I used to be a book
Now I am a book

All the endings say
All the dreams say

All the children say

* * *

Once upon a once there was a once
and that once evaporated into air
it was said it once was all over the sky
then once came back and died

It was said –

my smile is becoming a page
– becoming an adventure

It sang –

my smile is what the children say

Caption

But where are the snows of yester-year?
François Villon

One less body is lost in snow
The dying one (in time) becomes a landscape,
    do you remember how it came about?

Snow unlike glass, glass unlike a corpse
Moon unlike a torso boldly colored in
    with bark, with slate, with soil breaking up

in the furrows of another eroding shape

Or a severed line, bringing us together for the first time
March unlike Spring or an almanac out of date,
    nomenclature: everywhere

Evidence, perception, conclusion
Unlike a dull pool on a brown tire track,
    earlier I said landscape

How did it come about?

Grief unlike truth, truth unlike snow
Body unlike its outline

Pierced

The heart of poetry is fatigue
makes space around a toy majestic
opening night unto neglect, dark and neglect
the weight of that, the weight

at the heart is a great stillness in a tiny pocket

a rag folded lengthwise
placed over eyes
witness the crease a smile makes

a substantive kiss

at the heart, fatigue is a grimace
a gap between tooth & tongue
chance, love & logic
the scalpel & scripture
tent show, RENT-A-BENCH
& Chicken Little
that swell vista between the century and now
its faded bunting

come as you are

At the heart is a great harangue
rich with fatigue, a crowd of sighs
of difficult breath, fish mouth against sky

empty hands behind the high school

The heart of poetry is an angry child
a decaying spider in a chain link fence
a rotten cushion at the bottom of a stream
springs busted out, fabric torn
a shooting gallery in the basement

the heart of poetry is a ripped sock
covering that wound, fresh with it

the actual bone is bone

Take it as an experiment
where a voice can say
this face is pleasing, it has work in it
it is a building

just a song tweaking dawn

A youth, a maiden pledge themselves
'o we could be happy, o we could be...'
one step forward two steps back

>   Inside the song, it's weird
>   glue tears, and a trail of crumbs
>
>   Inside the sound, it's green
>   camphor & alabaster
>
>   Inside the spine, breath
>   stapled & sewn, a stem

the things protein does/was

The lungs are small and occupy the breast
the rest is a fable heard in the brush

whose home,
what letter,
what book?

whose tomb?

The heart of poetry is an empty lot
where the wind will not cease,

that particular volume of leaf wrack
and heat continues, contains much
as we make camp in its folds, that wind
distinct from any other hand

The pulse of these times is weak
an anonymous trick, tock
dirty knees and bruised biceps
a smudge below the lip
clavicle swollen from fists

The heart of poetry is a hollow man
a heteronym, a forensic test, & casino chip
a long distance call

when it comes the music is not the story
and the prodigal's song abides

beliefs dictate syntax

the diamond we let go
a mockingbird, a mulberry bush,
a dog-eared copy of the *Metamorphoses*
string of moon beyond industrial lot
'that wheel is rusted, the car – the windows –
are busted out'

The populist's vision dims
dented at the moment of ascendancy

is that all there is

There is a science to this song
even if they wasn't people to write

but the mind of a page is the form of a body
the one we touch, the one that makes laws

body of straw

m-m-moon, s-s-tring, br-r-anch
open the throat to recite

e-egg, t-twine, s-s-tick
open the throat to sing

to sigh, then sign the reply
turning words to return the world

here you are: t-t-tree, bowl of fruit
here it is: cello & lute
sun shaft in garden,   on dirt

the leafy plot is tenuous

The heart of poetry is fatigue
what the teachers left unsaid
a whimpering man inside the child
failed cathedral, overflowing shelter
a woman in the shape of a man
man in the shape of an animal
animal shape of a children's book
crust of bread
a skinny leg inside a blown-out shoe
at the side of an ocean
at the mouth of the delta
at the foot of a glacier
dung hill, mini mart
burial mound and parking lot
all sucked into a vacuum
the cartoon black spot
of an eye, a tiny pool of ink
through which the overload
overlord of images pour
into bodies uncensored
phantom of what we really are

a stain in the center of a field
grease spot on grass blade, on shirt

in the magazine 'a mother clutches the skull
of her actual daughter'

the graphic surface of objects' stink

And what difference would it make
if the face were projected
from the bole of an oak
to the tip of its crown
from the end of an alley
to the mouth of a creek
Were a body of water
become a plot of land
what could it mean?
If a torso were dissolved
into many grains of sand
or the hand composed
from a swarm of bees
would it tell us we are plural
we are bytes of sound
as if a cell were projected
onto a screen, a glass slide
into the night sky

what would it take to open
the door, to embrace
the porous creatures
as if for the first time
again like it never was
and will always be

ex more
in medias res

peeling the apple to its final essence of spring?

Questions: what is, what if,
how to, how can

to err, to wander/wonder, to drift

Questions: then if so, how come
where to, how far

'is this good ground soldier?'

Take the short wave past storefronts
through grasslands, the polluted river

find tires, find no one

it was always this peaceful here
always, the distance seems to say

even I, here, now

And what about the hands become obsolete
what about poetry, at the heart
a late breaking story
between tabloid and rib

but this keeps on writing
the waters and arbors just after impact

When the flakes break and fill the burning sky
we will find ourselves
on streets just like this one

The heart of poetry is

an arc between grass blade and gown
hovering beneath an eclipse

'this keeps on writing'

The sky participates in our diaries
H for silence and breath, before death

a good book
fake book
pillow book
& notebook

here is my instrument
last will and testament

Item: 1 locket, broken, its vowels stolen

Item: to give up loneliness, give up happiness
(poor *maudit*)

Item: 1 cock, 1 comb, another evening
a predictable event

two cars race to the horizon

Tous Les Matins du Monde

Goodness is hard on the body,
a distracted mind unable to doze in fitful sleep.
The dove rattles the mind into thinking
it has a body of thought – complete
& symbolic – the gray feathers perched
outside the pale cut square of silver.
Say then, we belong to that window,
that warble, and suddenly we belong too,
the silver car in the yard, even a tiny silver hammer.
All vehicles of travel
disclose the mind's need to wonder in perfect forms.
Even if the skiffsman don't come to this bed
to rock me to sleep – to wander the tired stones again
and worn teeth we remember to hold onto a world
for this life might not take us the whole way.
That shape of an idea, the concept, or *donnée*
travels farther than the instrument can register.
The spindle whirs beyond its order.
Something must be moving at incredible speed.
With pure speed I address you, reality.

A History of the Lyric

And this is no other
Place than where I am
                    W.S. Graham

OBJECTS IN MIRROR ARE CLOSER
THAN THEY APPEAR

they are right next to you
in the lanes, hugging a shoulder

*

they twitter in rafters
calling down to your mess

in rays, crescents

the white curled backs
of snapshots tucked in a frame

eyes of the dead

*

there is a gimbal lamp, ledger
a table of solid deal

clocks & militaria

a dirty blotter
its crusty bottle, a plume

*

there are beetles and boojum
specimen jars decorated

with walkingsticks, water striders
and luna moths

a treatise on rotating spheres

*

this swivel chair, worn
from some years past

a few doubloons, powder horn
musket bag and tricorne hat

a cannon, its yawning round

*

they are closer than comfort
closer than night breaking
over the mountain face

empurpled, its silhouette
ragged, silver

unquantifiable in pixie dusk

*

closer than power lines
casting shadows on brush

breath, heart ticking
the prepared delay

as twilight settles
in waves and crests

a water fowl, hooded owl

*

an avant-garde
a backward glance

to think I have written this poem before
to think to say the reason I came here
sound of yard bird, clinking lightbulb

to think the world has lasted this long

what were we hoping to say:
ailanthus, rosebud, gable
saturnalia, moonglow, remember

I am on the other side now
have crossed the river, have
through much difficulty
come to you from a dormer closet
head full of dark
my voice in what you say

at this moment you say
wind through stone, through teeth
through falling sheets, flapping geese

every thing is poetry here

a vast blank fronting the eyes
more sparkling than sun on brick
October's crossing-guard orange

Lateness is a dark and luminous thing
so true of early twilight.

I have known the morning to be darkest
upon waking. The pictures go away

and one is back to the thing of living.
Things to handle and attend:

Hawthorne, willow spear.

*

If the dark speaks what does it say
in a dark time. As words choose me

are they mine, and the counterpointing wind.
If a catalog inserted here, your name here.

If the road turned, if your erratum
came to naught (for *with* read wick,

for *tear* read torn), if you found me.

*

This night dissolves outlines – trees,
leaves and power lines along the way.

What way? The goodly silence
returns its music as lateness falling

falls back into nerve.

*

So things come together, one
and one. And if one, and if

an overwhelming sense of rescue:
fallen leaf. Broken acorn. Schoolyard tears.

A grandiosity for being useful:
burning ship. Buckling dam.

*

Jets report a mass of shaped sound
off beyond the tree line.

I wanted to go to it: if leaf beauty,
if cloud beauty, if ideas of relation.

that you are not among the winter branches
the door opening
a trapezoid in deep gold light
I awoke to water in the distance
rushing loud as traffic on High St.
more real than traffic on High St.
if you were to come now
hair draping your shoulders
were to kiss my neck
bending to clip the flower
a happy lover might be
known to run to excess
but tell me am I happy

I lost you to the inky noise
just offscreen that calls us

and partly we got stuck there
waving, walking into the Percy grass.

A sinking pictorial velvet spray
imagining vermilion dusk.

You lost me to your petticoat
shimmering armor

saying it is better here
on my own. Why

can't we or is it won't you
leave your solo ingle

beside the page. Did we never
consider life lyric interruption

to the idyll, laboring to rescue
real time, lost in affection.

Back roads dead-end in every epoch
but our view was singular, private

shared vistas of original walks.
Don't trade on this high tone

for silence, rather lumen chatter
recalling the better part of day.

CODA

When the sky came down
there was wind, water, red

When the sky fell
it became water, wind
a declaration in blue

When the end was near
I picked up for a moment, joy
came into my voice

Hurry up it sang
in skiffs and shafts
Selah in silvered tones

When the day broke open
I became myself
standing next to a door

In my dream you were alive
and crying

Overtakelessness

after Albert Pinkham Ryder

To speak inaudibly, the outside,
its blurred sentence foreshadowed,
indistinguishable as shining brass.
The room, the empty sky, beautiful
or golden bands burn because it is empty.
Without depth of field birds become primitive again.
Unstuck weeds float downstream
completing representation.
A thick green complicating light.
Now face the horizon in silence.
Come down while gladness unbinds sleep
unlike silt. This quiet speech feels right
and will be imitated. To turn away,
to speak fondly without a history.
Come down and rediscover this ancient province
as persons exchange smiles like wind instruments.
There, unlike any road you travel,
are small tidings that awakening,
are pleasing. No history is clear.

Edgar Poe

Winter's the thing.
A place to lay one's head.
To sleep at last

to sleep. Blue on flesh
in snow light,
iced boughs overhead.

This is a poem about breath,
brick, a piece of ink
in the distance.

Winter's the thing
I miss. The font is still.
A fanfare of stone air.

It Was Raining in Delft

A cornerstone. Marble pilings. Curbstones and brick.
I saw rooftops. The sun after a rain shower.
Liz, there are children in clumsy jackets. Cobblestones
    and the sun now in a curbside pool.
I will call in an hour where you are sleeping. I've been walking
    for 7 hrs on yr name day.
Dead, I am calling you now.
There are colonnades. Yellow wrappers in the square.
Just what you'd suspect: a market with flowers and matrons,
    handbags.
Beauty walks this world. It ages everything.
I am far and I am an animal and I am just another I-am poem,
    a we-see poem, a they-love poem.
The green. All the different windows.
There is so much stone here. And grass. So beautiful each
    translucent electric blade.
And the noise. Cheers folding into traffic. These things.
    Things that have been already said many times:
leaf, zipper, sparrow, lintel, scarf, window shade.

Château If

If love if then if now if the flowers of if the conditional
if of arrows the condition of if
    if to say light to inhabit light if to speak if to live, so
    if to say it is you if love is if your form is if your waist
that pictures the fluted stem if lavender
    if in this field
    if I were to say hummingbird it might behave as an
adjective here
    if not if the heart's a flutter if nerves map a city if a city
on fire
    if I say myself am I saying myself (if in this instant) as if
the object of your gaze if in a sentence about love you might
write if one day if you would, so
    if to say myself if in this instance if to speak as another –
    if only to render if in time and accept if to live now as if
disembodied from the actual handwritten letters m-y-s-e-l-f
    if a creature if what you say if only to embroider – a city
that overtakes the city I write.

Plain Song

Some say a baby cries for the life to come
some say leaves are green 'cause it looks good against
the blue
some say the grasses blow because it is earth's instru-
ment
some say we were born to cry

∗

Some say that the sun comes close every year because it
wants to be near us
some say the waters rise to meet it
others say the moon is our mother, *ma mère*

∗

Some say birds overhead are a calligraphy: every child
learning the words 'home'
some say that the land and the language are the father
some say the land is not ours
some say in time we'll rise to meet it

∗

Some say there are the rushes the geese the tributaries
and the reeds

∗

Some say the song of the dove is an emblem of thought
some say lightning and some the electric light some say
they are brothers

∗

Some say the current in the wall is the ground
some say the nervous system does not stop with the
body
some say the body does not stop

*

Some say beauty is only how you look at it and some
beauty is what we have some say there is no beauty some
truth

*

Some say the ground is stable
others the earth is round
for some it is a stone
I say the earth is porous and we fall constantly

*

Some say light rings some say that light is a wave some
say it has a weight or there is a heft to it

*

Some say all of these things and some say not
some say the way of the beekeeper is not their way
some say the way of the beekeeper is the only way
some say simple things all there are are simple things

*

Some say 'the good way', some 'stuff'
some say yes we need a form
some say form is a simple thing some say yes the sky is
a form of what is simple

*

Some say molecular some open others porous some
blue
    some say love some light some say the dark some
heaven

To Be Written in No Other Country

Now it is time for the scratch ticket
to bruise the inner wishes of single moms,
for night to be enough for the pensioner
and his 'Buster' in TV light.
If we were to answer the geese overhead
would we ever find a home
lost as we are in the kiddy section of Wal-Mart?
As a youth did Grant wonder
that he would become both a drunk
and president and die like Melville, forgotten,
buried under ambition and guilt.
It is a sorry day for the pollster and body electorate
for the mildewed pages of a wound dresser.
And when and whenever past Saturdays
of adolescents in faded Kodak
enter the discourse of politicians
know you are not alone and your scrapbook
will be enough in talk of resolutions
and what you plan to do this weekend
to the garage and to the porch.

Revival

for Gregory Corso (1930–2001)

It's good to be dead in America
with the movies, curtains and drift,
the muzak in the theater.
It's good to be in a theater waiting
for The Best Years of Our Lives to begin.
Our first night back, we're here
entertaining a hunch our plane did crash
somewhere over the Rockies, luggage
and manuscripts scattered, charred fragments
attempting to survive the fatal draft.
To be dead in America at the movies
distracted by preview music in dimming lights.
I never once thought of Alfred Deller
or Kathleen Ferrier singing Kindertotenlieder.
It's good to be lost among pillars of grass.
I never once thought of My Last Duchess
or the Pines of Rome. Isn't it great here
just now dying along with azaleas, trilliums,
myrtle, viburnums, daffodils, blue phlox?
It's good to be a ghost in America,
light flooding in at this moment
of never coming back to the same person
who knew certain things, certain people,
shafts of life entering a kitchen
at the end of an age of never coming back now.
To hear reports on the radio,
something about speed, they say, accelerated history.
It's good to share molecular chasm with a friend.
I never once reached for Heisenberg
or The Fall of the Roman Empire.

On this day in history the first antelope was born,
remember The Yearling, like that,
but the footage distressed, handheld.

A hard, closed, linear world at the edge
of caricature, no memory now of the New Science
or The Origin of the Species.
It's good to feel hunted in America.
To be the son of a large man who rose out of depression
and the middle world war, poverty and race
to loom in mid-sixties industrial American air,
survived classic notions of the atom,
to think to be. The official story walks
down the street, enters bars and cafes.
Plays. Airs. Stars. To sing a song of industry,
having forgotten Monty Clift was beaten
for reading Ulysses. It's dark in a theater,
hoping to say never return to the moment
of return, as a hollow ring from Apollo 13
sinks back to burn into the atmosphere
which made it, huh. How come all the best thoughts
are images? How come all the best images
are uncanny? What's the use of The Compleat Angler,
searching for effects at the bottom of a lake
next to a shoe slick with algae, at the base of a cliff
with pine needles and a rotting log?

I was talking about rending, reading, rewriting
what is seen. Put the book down and look into the day.
I want an art that can say how I am feeling
if I am feeling blue sky unrolling a coronation rug
unto the bare toe of a peasant girl
with vague memories of Jeanne d'Arc,
or that transformation in Cinderella.
Where is your mother today?
I think of you, soft skin against soot.
How much has the world turned
since you were a girl in Troy?
In these parts both widow and banker are diminished,
something outside the town defeated them.
In these parts neither possessed their life.
This pageant demands too much,

that we work and not break, that we love
and not lie, and not complain.
It's good to not break in America.
To behave this time
never once looking into Chapman's Homer,
or quoting the Vita Nuova translated
by Dante Rossetti. No, I am thinking
blurry faces, a boy, girl, looking
at New York harbor for a first time,
soil in pockets, missing buttons,
needing glasses, needing shoes.

It was war. A capital experience!
Investing in narratives of working up
from the mail room, basement, kitchen.
It's good to believe in the press kit
sailing away from rear-projection tenements
like a car ride after a good fix,
offset by attractively angled shots,
neo-cartoonish, with massive distorting close-ups,
part lockdown, part interest rate,
part plant, part machine. Part dazzle?
Lulls and high sensations.
I always wished I could be funny ha-ha,
instead of 'he's a little funny', if you get my drift,
just courage to accept the facts
that poetry can catch you in the headlights
and it's years refocusing the afterimage,
the depth and passion of its earnest glance.
This part untranslatable, part missing line,
feather in the chest. A description
to account for the lack of detail
the Wealth of Nations conducts on the organs.
We look forward to serving you here
at Managed Health Network.
Thank you for calling, call volume
is still exceptionally heavy. If this is an emergency…

All the codes have been compromised.
This is why the boy can't fathom polar lights,
liberty, merry dancer.
Ineluctably the privileged nostalgia of a toy boat.
In the diagram did the vessel survive?
Like an old book, even a beloved book,
its pages give way to a good sneeze.
What have they done, I sit here thinking
of your monuments, trophies, hahahaha.
'Here are my flowers',
what do they smell like? 'Paper.'
This is why athenaeum joy, why shiny pathos
intoning the letters, prance and skater,
o say, can you see?
What does it mean to wait for a song
to sit and wait for a story?
For want of a sound to call my own
coming in over the barricades,
to collect rubble at the perimeter
hoping to build a house, part snow, part victory,
ice and sun balancing the untrained shafts,
part sheet music, part dust, sings often –
the parts open, flake, break open, let go.
Why so phantom, searching for a rag
to embellish the holes in my sonnet,
no tracks leading beyond and back,
no more retrograde song cycle tatting air.
These parts wobble, stitching frames
to improvise a document:
all this American life. Strike that.
All our life, all our American lives gathered
into an anthem we thought to rescue us,
over and out. On your way, dust.

In Defense of Nothing

I guess these trailers lined up in the lot off the highway will do.
I guess that crooked eucalyptus tree also.
I guess this highway will have to do and the cars
    and the people in them on their way.
The present is always coming up to us, surrounding us.
It's hard to imagine atoms, hard to imagine
    hydrogen & oxygen binding, it'll have to do.
This sky with its macular clouds also
    and that electric tower to the left, one line broken free.

Beginning with a Phrase from Simone Weil

There is no better time than the present when we have
lost everything. It doesn't mean rain falling
   at a certain declension, at a variable speed is without
purpose or design.
   The present everything is lost in time, according to laws
of physics things shift
      when we lose sight of a present,
      when there is no more everything. No more presence in
everything loved.

In the expanding model things slowly drift and
everything better than the present is lost in no time.
   A day mulches according to gravity
   and the sow bug marches. Gone, the hinge cracks, the
gate swings a breeze,
      breeze contingent upon a grace opening to air,
      velocity tied to winging clay. Every anything in its
peculiar station.

The sun brightens as it bleaches, fades the spectral value
in everything seen. And chaos is no better model
   when we come adrift.
   When we have lost a presence when there is no more
everything. No more presence in everything loved,
      losing anything to the present. I heard a fly buzz. I
heard revealed nature,
      cars in the street and the garbage, footprints of a world,
every fly a perpetual window,
      unalloyed life, *gling*, pinnacles of tar.

There is no better everything than loss when we have
time. No lack in the present better than everything.
In this expanding model rain falls
according to laws of physics, things drift. And every-
thing better than the present is gone
in no time. A certain declension, a variable speed.
Is there no better presence than loss?
A grace opening to air.
No better time than the present.

A Panic That Can Still Come Upon Me

If today and today I am calling aloud

If I break into pieces of glitter on asphalt
bits of sun, the din

if tires whine on wet pavement
everything humming

If we find we are still in motion
and have arrived in Zeno's thought, like

if sunshine hits marble and the sea lights up
we might know we were loved, are loved
if flames and harvest, the enchanted plain

If our wishes are met with dirt
and thyme, thistle, oil,
heirloom, and basil

or the end result is worry, chaos
and if 'I should know better'

If our loves are anointed with missiles
Apache fire, Tomahawks
did we follow the tablets the pilgrims suggested

If we ask that every song touch its origin
just once and the years engulfed

If problems of identity confound sages,
derelict philosophers, administrators
who can say I am found

if this time you, all of it, this time now

If nothing save Saturdays at the metro and
if rain falls sidelong in the platz
doorways, onto mansard roofs

If enumerations of the fall
and if falling, cities rocked
with gas fires at dawn

Can you rescind the ghost's double nakedness
hungry and waning

if children, soldiers, children
taken down in schools

if burning fuel

Who can't say they have seen this
and can we sing this

if in the auroras' reflecting the sea,
gauze touching the breast

Too bad for you, beautiful singer
unadorned by laurel
child of thunder and scapegoat alike

If the crowd in the mind becoming
crowded in streets and villages, and trains
run next to the freeway

If exit is merely a sign

2.

It isn't alright to want just anything
all the time, be specific sky

I can read the narrow line above the hills

The day unbraids its pretty light
and I am here to see it

This must be all there is
right now in the world

There are things larger than understanding

things we know cannot
be held in the mind

If the sun throbs like a drum
every five minutes

what can we do with this

the 100,000 years it takes a photon
to reach the surface of the sun

eight minutes to hit our eyes

If every afternoon gravity and fire
it's like that here

undressed, unwound

3.

If today and today I am speaking to you, or
if you/I whisper, touch, explain

If they/you hate those phrases
if we struggle to get to the thing
the body and the other noises

If a W stumbles here even in private
there was this man we said
everywhere between us

if speech can free us

If summer fall winter spring
the broadcast day spins round my head
its grin stuck out there

when I am a tiger inside the DMZ
or if I am a tiger man
if no one believes what I see

If behind the grail and new elm
the pink light saying welcome earthling

my biography as an atom
picture of my smile

is this what my body said

If I forget my notebook
if these gaps I feel are also the gaps
I am built inside, thinking it's all good

If the sun sharp and hot and still
but deep and clarifying, walking its boulevards

if bound by the most ignoble cords
if squatting in time

If every day a struggle, the blue copse speaking
sky arching over nothing – uh-huh

If every struggle ice-cream truck tinkle
interrupting the cosmological

if everyday strife, everyday *sprecenze*
if everyday uh

is this what my body says
my buddy said

and if I die
and begin to lose consciousness
and the flag

There was this man we said
this W here even in private

I said in my letter
if I see you again

4.

A branch and the scent of pine in summer
the bridge and the water in the creek
the stones and the sound of water
the creek and my body
when hair and water flowed over me

If I am a bridge I am standing on, thinking,
saying goodbye to myself
when I stood by the water in life
thinking of my life, pine boughs
the hill next to water

The sun in the creek on the bridge
on my hair and pine boughs
in wind mixed with water,
one crow skating by, the life
of water, life of thinking
and moving, a crow passes by
this place in the mind, on my eyes

5.

So the vocalise day imprinted a sound

I'm not stupid
I too unwind in the most circuitous fashion
I undress water directly

Who hasn't seen unnumbered sparrows
enter the silhouette of a tree

why shouldn't I come in from the cold

Sure, there is the monument
the grass and the plate it grows on

If the answer becomes sun
then sun inside, normal things, okay

the ribbon above our heads is not a banner

Scaling this leafy architecture
we say wind / night sky / moon / clouds / stars
if silver stands for syncopation

indeed, symphonic dailiness is felt order

I have felt it at the back of me,
light on the table, the book open

If we struggle for a name
if colors change

if mood is connected to naming, to color

If say a ship's in deep water
and a piece of sky empties the mind

or when I was frigate-tossed

if I wanted to go all over a word
and live inside its name, so be it

There is my body and the idea of my body
the surf breaking and the picture of a wave

The Outernationale

The sun deploys its shadows
and things grow in dark too.
Leaves arch over everything
they are so democratic
to us our viewer in a world of secrets
in a world of navigable
foreshortening emotional registers.
In the park, breeze-shaken
wrappers drift outward.
The sand here seems coliseum-like
it is so contesting
just plain old.
Who can we turn toward
walking the hills' unbridled shoulders
breathless far from the story?
The day blooms in its self-knowledge.
It's that simple when we ask about faith.
How can I answer
not to inhibit
any single point in this ray?
Out of this house and out into the day
things come to focus
silver-tipped antennae tweak the blue
and sheets of rainwater
at the foot of the statehouse.
Something is something
when the administration
of money flows backward.
In this word time seems a trip,
come back, little sheen of products
in rows behind glass.
We went to the store and why not
we go to the moon
jeweled box on a shelf.
In summer we open and opening

we wander and
before we were happy
we were unhappy.
Such is the dialectical
awakening everyone
is hankering to embrace.
When the TV's on
the faces in the stands echo
and bounce far into the field.
The hopes and suspense
so often submarine
made plain as a runner rounding 2nd.
There is reason to watch
unlike the blinking reflection
in a darkened window glass.
We find purpose
in the game and together,
this crucial passage given flight
when detail disappears into a crowd
that too quickly invested
and then discarded power.
It's getting dark
indigo setting on the glass
just sitting there. Reminding us
days gallop into grass rushing wind
into miles of cable.
When the pistons call,
when I was a wedge of sun
over steel mills,
when I asked what happened
I meant what happened to us?

Stung

A child I became a question
sitting on the grass.
To be told how lucky I am.
An open field.
This corporeal expanse
was a body too
in silver magnetism.
If I became this light
it wasn't luck. It was easy.
Bells falling away
along the divide of night.
Along the divide of night
an old face. A sorry dormer
leaning in askew
below the incoming thunder.
This was true and even if ever
I ran away. I ran
away. Above everything
I held one true thing.
This scene moved through me,
a seesaw. A picture
inside a question inside
the coming night.
These trees rang
round my head, shored
up the sky. I went on
and on like a trial balloon
over the houses. Over
the roofs. Over my head.

*

To remember correctly
the color of pale grass in March,

its salt hay blonde flourish.
To see it as it was,
faded cloth, mute trumpet,
the seam inside a day
the sun climbs.
Simple the life of the mind
standing outside in the grass
in March. Outside memory.
Spring interrupts
one cardinal monody
transmuted by a signal red
developed against
a draining blue horizon.
To want to go there
and to have been there
and to be there now.
This walking right now
by a river, simple and not so clear
when transcribing this
unstable multiplying narrative spring.
It can't be called anything.
We too are sprung and wound
with evolution, I want to say.
That's it: love. Not spring.
I have felt it also
in quilted drowning snow
under the sheets
in a clanking house.
Clank, I love you.
Clank. Not spring.
Glossy grass wigging
in a brightening sky.
The thrill of hair
standing on my limbs.

*

To be and not to understand.
To understand nothing
and be content
to watch light against
leaf-shadowed ground.
To accept the ground.
To go to it as a question.
To open up the day inside the day,
a bubble holding air
bending the vista to it.
To be inside this thing,
outside in the grass place,
out in the day
inside another thing.

Untitled Amherst Specter

a sound of open ground having been taken

now a silver wisp winking on the roof

silver imp waving from a long shaft ago

I am a leaf storm night

I have seen the long file of mule trains and metal

the cavalry

these sounds we live within speaking to you now

sir, I was a soldier in these woods

A Telescope Protects Its View

I like to read the dead.

Part of a whole lost era campaign.

The bridge is up.

A portrait of you from what you aren't saying.

On my sleeve. The verb to be.

I'm plucky but thankful.

Death and the imagination equals life itself.

Letters from an old bottle,
junk in space.

A book or a boat?

The black ribbons of a spring day
might sound mawkish

but I like to read under a pale blue sky
animated and deepening.

I like to read the dead.

There's so and so going by
everyone, outside

everyone

the words scroll onto air.

Synecdoche: act of receiving from another.

Metonymy: change of name.

Who hasn't found themselves
praying in an awkward room.

She said but what of their sad work
by the river's edge

sad way of working the moth paper light

trellis of dented garbage cans
and debris at dawn.

Human Memory Is Organic

We know time is a wave.

You can see it in gneiss, migmatic
or otherwise, everything crumbles.

Don't despair.

That's the message frozen in old stone.

I am just a visitor to this world
an interloper really headed deep into glass.

I, moving across a vast expanse of water

though it is not water maybe salt
or consciousness itself

enacted as empathy. Enacted as seeing.

To see with a purpose has its bloom
and falls to seed and returns

to be a story like any other.
To be a story open and vulnerable

a measure of time, a day, this day one might say
an angle of light for instance.

Let us examine green. Let us go together

to see it all unstable and becoming
violent and testing gravity

so natural in its hunger.

The organic existence of gravity.
The organic nature of history.

The natural history of tears.

Saturday and Its Festooned Potential

for Barbara Guest

Faces unlike weather
never return
no matter how closely
they resemble rain

In this theater, time
isn't cruel, just different

Does that help?

When the overgrown skyway
becomes calm
humans get quiet

When the notion of myth
or collective anything
is undone by wind chimes
by a gentle tink tink

When the mind is opened forth
by a gentle tink tink
or light speckled
and whooping in the periphery

When light whooping
and speckled is most pleasing
to a body at rest

When thought, open
attaches itself to repose
to the forehead

When twigs swaying
just outside
the library's large glass
signal, scratch, and join
to an idea of history

When twigs scratching
join to an idea of time
to a picture of being

Like to be beside and becoming
to be another and oneself
to be complete inside the poem

To be oneself becoming a poem

Vincent, Homesick for the Land of Pictures

Is this what you intended, Vincent
that we take our rest at the end of the grove
nestled into our portion beneath the bird's migration
saying, who and how am I made better through struggle.
Or why am I I inside this empty arboretum
this inward spiral of whoop ass and vision
the leafy vine twisting and choking the tree.
O, dear heaven, if you are indeed that
or if you can indeed hear what I might say
heal me and grant me laughter's bounty
of eyes and smiles, of eyes and affection.

To not be naive and think of silly answers only
nor to imagine answers would be the only destination
nor is questioning color even useful now
now that the white ray in the distant tree beacons.
That the sun can do this to us, every one of us
that the sun can do this to everything inside
the broken light refracted through leaves.
What the ancients called peace, no clearer example
what our fathers called the good, what better celebration.
Leaves shine in the body and in the head alike
the sun touches deeper than thought.

O to be useful, of use, to the actual seen thing
to be in some way related by one's actions in the world.
There might be nothing greater than this
nothing truer to the good feelings that vibrate within
like in the middle of the flower I call your name.
To correspond, to be in equanimity with organic stuff
to toil and to reflect and to home and to paint
father, and further, the migration of things.
The homing action of geese and wood mice.
The ample evidence of the sun inside all life
inside all life seen and felt and all the atomic pieces too.

But felt things exist in shadow, let us reflect.
The darkness bears a shine as yet unpunished by clarity
but perhaps a depth that outshines clarity and is true.
The dark is close to doubt and therefore close to the sun
at least what the old books called science or bowed down to.
The dark is not evil for it has indigo and cobalt inside
and let us never forget indigo and the warmth of that
the warmth of the mind reflected in a dark time
in the time of pictures and refracted light.
Ah, the sun is here too in the polar region of night
the animal proximity of another and of nigh.

To step into it as into a large surf in late August
to go out underneath it all above and sparkling.
To wonder and to dream and to look up at it
wondrous and strange companion to all our days
and the toil and worry and animal fear always with us.
The night sky, the deep sense of space, actual bodies of light
the gemstone brushstrokes in rays and shimmers
to be held tight, wound tighter in the act of seeing.
The sheer vertical act of feeling caught up in it
the sky, the moon, the many heavenly forms
these starry nights alone and connected alive at the edge.

Now to think of the silver and the almost blue in pewter.
To feel these hues down deep, feel color wax and wane
and yellow, yellows are the tonality of work and bread.
The deep abiding sun touching down and making its impression
making so much more of itself here than where it signals
the great burning orb installed at the center of each and every thing.
Isn't it comforting this notion of each and every thing
though nothing might be the final and actual expression of it
that nothing at the center of something alive and burning
green then mint, blue then shale, gray and gray into violet
into luminous dusk into dust then scattered now gone.

But what is the use now of this narrow ray, this door ajar
the narrow path canopied in dense wood calling
what of the striated purposelessness in lapidary shading and line.
To move on, to push forward, to take the next step, to die.
The circles grow large and ripple in the hatch-marked forever
the circle on the horizon rolling over and over into paint
into the not near, the now far, the distant long-off line of daylight.
That light was my enemy and one great source of agony
one great solace in paint and brotherhood the sky and grass.
The fragrant hills spoke in flowering tones I could hear
the gnarled cut stumps tearing the sky, eating the sun.

The gnarled cut stumps tearing the sky, eating the sun
the fragrant hills spoke in flowering tones I could hear
one great solace in paint and brotherhood the sky and grass.
That light was my enemy and one great source of agony
into the not near, the now far, the distant long-off line of daylight
the circle on the horizon rolling over and over into paint.
The circles grow large and ripple in the hatch-marked forever.
To move on, to push forward, to take the next step, to die.
What of the striated purposelessness in lapidary shading and line
the narrow path canopied in dense wood calling
but what is the use now of this narrow ray, this door ajar.

Into luminous dusk into dust then scattered now gone
green then mint, blue then shale, gray and gray into violet
that nothing at the center of something alive and burning
though nothing might be the final and actual expression of it.
Isn't it comforting this notion of each and every thing
the great burning orb installed at the center of each and every thing
making so much more of itself here than where it signals.
The deep abiding sun touching down and making its impression
and yellow, yellows are the tonality of work and bread.
To feel these hues down deep, feel color wax and wane
now to think of the silver and the almost blue in pewter.

These starry nights alone and connected alive at the edge
the sky, the moon, the many heavenly forms
the sheer vertical act of feeling caught up in it.
To be held tight, wound tighter in the act of seeing
the gemstone brushstrokes in rays and shimmers.
The night sky, the deep sense of space, actual bodies of light
and the toil and worry and animal fear always with us
wondrous and strange companion to all our days.
To wonder and to dream and to look up at it
to go out underneath it all above and sparkling
to step into it as into a large surf in late August.

The animal proximity of another and of nigh.
Ah, the sun is here too in the polar region of night
in the time of pictures and refracted light
the warmth of the mind reflected in a dark time
and let us never forget indigo and the warmth of that.
The dark is not evil for it has indigo and cobalt inside
at least what the old books called science or bowed down to.
The dark is close to doubt and therefore close to the sun
but perhaps a depth that outshines clarity and is true.
The darkness bears a shine as yet unpunished by clarity
but felt things exist in shadow, let us reflect.

Inside all life seen and felt and all the atomic pieces too
the ample evidence of the sun inside all life
the homing action of geese and wood mice
father, and further, the migration of things.
To toil and to reflect and to home and to paint
to correspond, to be in equanimity with organic stuff
like in the middle of the flower I call your name.
Nothing truer to the good feelings that vibrate within
there might be nothing greater than this
to be in some way related by one's actions in the world.
O to be useful, of use, to the actual seen thing.

The sun touches deeper than thought
leaves shine in the body and in the head alike
what our fathers called the good, what better celebration.
What the ancients called peace, no clearer example
the broken light refracted through leaves.
That the sun can do this to everything inside
that the sun can do this to us, every one of us
now that the white ray in the distant tree beacons.
Nor is questioning color even useful now
nor to imagine answers would be the only destination
to not be naive and think of silly answers only.

Of eyes and smiles, of eyes and affection
heal me and grant me laughter's bounty.
Or if you can indeed hear what I might say
O, dear heaven, if you are indeed that
the leafy vine twisting and choking the tree
this inward spiral of whoop ass and vision.
Or why am I I inside this empty arboretum
saying, who and how am I made better through struggle
nestled into our portion beneath the bird's migration
that we take our rest at the end of the grove
is this what you intended, Vincent.

Wintry Mix

The 6 a.m. January
encaustic clouds
are built
in a waxy gray putty
whizzing by with spots
of luminous silvery
crack-o'-the-world light
coming through, an eerie
end-o'-the-world feeling
yet reassuring
like an old movie.
Do I really have to go out there?
Now a hint of muted
salmon tones breaking
a warmish band
of welcoming pinkish light.
Is it like this every morning?
My head still in the dark.
Worry, eck! But the brightening
russet tipped cloud ballet
reminds me of something
in Pliny, yeah, Pliny.
Can't imagine opening
the door today in a toga.
Work and more,
yes, work
sends us into the draft.

Bolshevescent

You stand far from the crowd, adjacent to power.
You consider the edge as well as the frame.
You consider beauty, depth of field, lighting
to understand the field, the crowd.
Late into the day, the atmosphere explodes
and revolution, well, revolution is everything.
You begin to see for the first time
everything is just like the last thing
only its opposite and only for a moment.
When a revolution completes its orbit
the objects return only different
for having stayed the same throughout.
To continue is not what you imagined.
But what you imagined was to change
and so you have and so has the crowd.

The Outernationale

One has emotions for the strangest things.
W.C. Williams, *Kora in Hell*

So the bird's in the hand
and now what?
The penny shiny
in the dark belly of mr piggy.
The day dawns and dawns
and may be in trouble
of actually going anywhere.
Trees migrate secretly up-
ward. They might be saying
all we need to be here
if we would only stop
talking and listen up.
I love you, said the wood.
One sonic color into
the egregious public air.
Start from nothing and be-
long to it. The signal
and its noise -itsy,
-ancy, -oid.
So many strangers
alive in a larynx.
So much depends on X
so much more
on the book in your hand.
Start from nothing
and let the sound reach you.

There is that field
in the window once again
and to write of this field
again is certainly a failure
of any inward rigor

or life. To live certainly
on the surface -ing, -ed, or
things pinging off
the metal empty core
scrolling for a perfect tune
to cue the mood
outraged or bittersweet,
vintage etc. and emptier
than the supra-empty
of the mood stabilizer
flat line -less, -let
-like, -ly. The cold parts
of the car body.
Why can't I just admit
I'm dead, have been dead
since I met me, -metry, -ality
unseen and undone
by the no time
I was raised into
out of the incubator
-obic, -etic, -istic
the stain of the world
got on me.
You see it on TV.
Everyday weather
and the everyday weatherman.
The car racing
into a slow fade.
Rain opening the next shot,
falling everywhere
around the boy falling digitally
just now as you read this.
It is always raining
in pictures, inside
this feeling of mercy
-ency, -esse
or this writing along the edge
which is of course

writing about hope
if we could only open
our hardware
to rewrite the software
down deep, the body
coming to, inside
this wooden structure
-archy, -ology, -ocracy.

Skylark, do you
have anything
to say to me?

Have you come
as a flower on the hill?

I am beside you
alive in the folds
of your parka.

Have you a single
new idea? Yes,
I carry the oldest ones.

Who will live
inside the song?

Is it only sand?
The voice of sand
-mandias, -icious, -rex.

The box is spitting electro-
magnetic lies into the room
again. I get sick and weak
just gawking to find
myself already full
of onions and laughter
-illiant, -ismus, arrogance.

I don't want to go there.
Don't want the lockdown
the bray, the cobbled headgear.
Can't it be clear? Can't it?
So often the inklings
the starter round
the jerk and huh of morning.
But the instants, the lake walks
and for a *blip* open sky
unshackling a bad history.
Nothing more personal
than headlines.
But what of the colors
in the new season sky?
It is only where
spring and death meet
-sic, -cide, -ulation.
Who says we are lacking
in courage?

The most forgotten history
is often the best. Best?
Ruined tar paper
against brick factory lots,
brick, brick,
smokestack, sky.
Even the light fades badly.
These old windows
bend the world.
I could never find
my way there and now
we are only here.
That's something
more than spectacular sunsets,
fading shafts on water.
With each one dies a world.
Or an empty casement
letting light in

bricolaged, alive for a moment
and then obfuscation
of late afternoon.
If only I knew then
what I know to be
outside my head
rain-washed and open.
Can't one stumble beyond
the cheap effects
of planet light, planet tilt
and all that google?

Once the sweet laughter
of indestructibility
cackled from my mouth.
No hiding the pain
my body was in space
and the empathy borne
of earthly gravity
earthly sentience
weighted to the bed,
the floor, the street,
the planet, -mania,
-polis, -ment.
Such cruelty comes
from lack of everything
or so I imagined,
having failed
to save anyone
from anything
in this empty house.
From this empty empty house
in first dull winter light
staring hard into spackle.
How could I save anyone
from the truly gnarly
unnecessary -osis
of a steel wind off a boulevard

rich with dog shit and perfume
carbon monoxide and subway grates
the confusion of sex and death
of childhood and decay
of sideway glances and
dinnish noises
of all things dented
and almost destroyed
amidst the once of beauty
and ankle bracelets.
The whole wide whorl
of economics charted
on a dart board
in bed sheets, -th,
-onomy, -illion, -ation.

The time to breathe
is now, there will be no time
to think but perhaps
you have no doubt.
I would like
to expose doubt itself
to open up
the mechanics of want
-ivorous, -etic, -esque, so
someone can feel it.
So someone can feel it
and break it down
inside themselves.
To rip out the gears
and belts, to empty
once and for all expectation,
the guitar sound
of young adult life
-ectric, -philia, -phyte.
The radio backdrop
speckled and moving.
The car window specked

and the sky moving.
The neighborhood
coming into view.
So the new poverty is just
like the old poverty.
The system has been upgraded
but the light, dishwater,
is mucking up the mood.
Whoever said
absolute powerlessness
corrupts absolutely?
Does it get any better?
Jeweled spots, translucent
over the windshield,
now pierced in white stinging
-hood, -holic, -hedron.
The cellular body
fuzzed out in sun,
oversaturated in Polaroid
reddish brown.
Where are we going
in the mechanical seconds
of this handheld movie,
this color that touches down?

If we could say
the world has changed,
it has changed. If we say
the world is the same
then so it is. But nothing
changes everything.
Even the beloved
evolves into −ust,
-est, -unction, -iction.
For all its iron and science
a bridge expands over foliage.
The river dappled
with wind and speed

and the sensation of night.
Throw back your head
to the milky tears.
All types and shapes
of silent light.
Here the crab, the bear,
the dipper, the wheel
and the little tightnesses
that keep us wanting.
The wanting that keeps us
looking hard into the dark.
The dark we hope to unpack
and move into
that one day
we might find ourselves lit up.

The Growing Edge

There is a spike
in the air
a distant thrum
you call singing
and how many nights
this giganto, torn
tuned, I wonder if
you hear me
I mean I talk
to myself through you
hectoring air
you're out there
tonight and so am I
for as long as
I remember
I talk to the air
what is it
to be tough
what ever
do you mean
how mistaken
can I be, how
did I miss it
as I do entirely
and admit very
well then
I know nothing
of the world
can see it now
can really see
there is a spike
a distant thrum
to the empty
o'clock autumn litter
it's ominous, gratuitous

the asphalt quality
these feelings
it's Sunday in deep space
and in the breeze
scatters, felt presences
behind the hole
in the day, sparks
ominous spike
I've not been here
before, my voice is
looking for a door
this offing light
reaching into maw
what does it mean
to enter that room
the last time
I remembered it
an *un* gathering
every piece of
open sky into it
the deep chill
inventing, and
is it comfort
the cold returning
now clear and
crystalline cold
I standing
feet on the ground
I frozen and
I can feel it
to meet incumbent
death we carry
within us a body
frozen ground
what does it mean
to be tough
or to write a poem
I mean the whole

vortex of home
buckling inside
a deep sea whine
flash lightning
birth storms
weather of pale
blinding life

Hypostasis & New Year

For why am I afraid to sing
the fundamental shape of awe
should I now begin to sing the silvered back of
    the winter willow spear
the sparkling agate blue
would this blade and this sky free me to speak
    intransitive lack –

the vowels themselves free

Of what am I afraid
of what lies in back of me of day
these stars scattered as far as the I
what world and wherefore
will it shake free
why now in the mind of an afternoon is a daisy
    for a while
flagrant and alive

Then what of night
of hours' unpredicated bad luck and the rot
    it clings to
fathomless on the far side in winter dark
Hey shadow world when a thing comes back
comes back unseen but felt and no longer itself
    what then
what silver world mirrors tarnished lenses
what fortune what fate
and the forms not themselves but only itself the sky
by water and wind shaken
I am born in silvered dark

Of what am I to see these things between myself
    and nothing
between the curtain and the stain

between the hypostatic scenes of breathing
and becoming the thing I see
are they not the same

Things don't look good on the street today
beside a tower in a rusting lot
one is a condition the other mystery
even this afternoon light so kind and nourishing
a towering absence vibrating air

Shake and I see pots from old shake
        and I see cities anew
I see robes shake I see desert
I see the farthing in us all the ghost of day
the day inside night as tones decay
        and border air
it is the old songs and the present wind I sing
and say I love the unknown sound in a word

Mother where from did you leave me on the sleeve
        of a dying word
of impish laughter in the midst my joy
I compel and confess open form
my cracked hinged picture doubled

I can't remember now if I made a pact with the devil
        when I was young
when I was high
on a sidewalk I hear 'buy a sweatshirt?' and think
buy a shirt from the sweat of children
        hell
I'm just taking a walk in the sun in a poem
        and this sound
caught in the most recent coup

Eye of the Poem

I come to it at an edge
morphed and hobbled,
still morphing. There is also
the blowtorch grammar's
unconquered flame.
That may sound laughable
but we'll need strength.
We'll need the willow's flex,
the flapping windsock.
We'll need every bit
of solar wind, serious goggles.

This is the snow channel
and it's snowing. Hey,
you wanted throttle,
you wanted full bore.
Stay open to adventure.
Being awake is finally
a comprehensive joy.
Stay open to that nimbus
around the back porch reverie,
every parti-colored aura
on cars left and to the right of you.

Ascending through the core
I am silly with clarity.
Born of air I am and
the dappled buttresses
in this vacuum glisten.
I remake my life.
What pressure animating giddy coil.
What not the flutter, every
ting and flange calling to you.
A bright patch over the roof
on the jobsite singing itself.

Analemma

That I came back to live
in the region both
my parents died into
that I will die into
if I have nothing else
I have this and
it's not morbid
to think this way
to see things in time
to understand I'll be gone
that the future is already
some where
I'm in that somewhere
and what of it
it's ok to see these things
to be the way they are
I can be them
have been them
will be there, soon
I know why I came here
to be back here
where my parents went
I know that I'll be there
to join them soon
it's ok to think this way
why shouldn't I
whose gonna say I shouldn't
a doctor, some friend
I have no wife in this
at night, late, the dark
myself at the ceiling
the arguments continue
I'm with it, it's with me
I am *quelque chose*
something with birds in it

a storm high above Albany
I am ghost brain I
sister to all things cruelty
the mouse-back gray
of every afternoon
and your sorrowing
now that you're gone
and I'm here or now
that you're here and
I'm gone or now
that you're gone and
I'm gone what
did we learn
what did we take
from that oh
always dilating
now that you're here
and also gone
I am just learning
that threshold
and changing light
a leafy-shaped blue
drifting above
an upstate New York
Mohican light
a tungsten light
boxcar lights
an oaken table-rapping
archival light
burnt over, shaking

Basement Song

Out of the deep
I dreamt the mother.

How deep the mother
deep the basement

the body, odor of laundry
the soul of a bug.

The grass inside
the song stains me.

The mother stains me.
That was the year

they cut my throat
and toads bloomed

on my voice box.
I have kept my head up.

Have kept myself
out of trouble

but deep is trouble
deep is mother.

Deep the song
inside summer.

Did I tell you it hurt
accepting air in a new body?

And since the change
the air burns.

Fragment

When you wake to brick outside the window

when you accept this handmade world

when you see yourself inside and accept its picture

when you feel the planet spin, accelerate, make dust
  of everything beneath your bed

when you say I want to live and the light that breaks
  is an inward light

when you feel speed of days, speed of light

if one could fancy vision then let it be of you

let it be thought breaking in your view

Pinocchio's Gnosis

The season folds into itself, cuts a notch in me. I become thinner. My heart splinters and a wooden sound invades the song, interrupts my ire. Today the planet is mostly dirt, mostly water – forget about my lyre. And if you look close everywhere coming to the surface, bare trees, bare yard showing through.

*

The wind is blowing west. The wind leaning, the trees sway, the clouds there. Grief is an undersong, it has its region naturally like a river valley spilling over like a nest inside the inside of feeling. Roughed. Go west originally came from ghost stories and not the campfire kind but a real ghost and a real story bleeding.

*

In my father's house I killed a cricket with an old sole. Funny how being dead troubles the word. I am trying to untie this sentence, to untidy the rooms where we live. No words in the soup, no soup in this sky, no more history written onto onionskin, peeling onion skins.

*

If I decide to laugh all the time I'll surely rid myself of tears. Why accept less than a joke, teasing lone from the lonely, bending the guy into guidebook. Hey you, Mr. *Sacer interpresque deorum*, how about a good bray, a laugh track in sync with your lyre? No?

*

Tears too form a roaring truth on the rolling green. Sure it's a nice day. A splendid day when joy met doom, the entire forest wept. Is not the tree more beautiful than the wood, the crown more lovely than the grain? There is an order. Small things assert themselves.

★

Once we understood velvet suggested elegance and distinction or my ruddy cheeks were more chevalier than clown or sawdust, din and clatter, tin cymbal. But today you have no joy for yesterday's plaything. Sumptuous velvet has lost its bloom. The rider is now that 'funny man', his ceaseless chatter.

★

All the world's a stooge. The secret and silent world worn from abuse and those surfaces abrading imagination. The patient world of the abandoned daydream so gay and corrosive. We have entered the semantics of useless things.

★

I am trying to untie the anvil sitting on my head I call my heart. This is a new sensation. I mean sing song bang bang behind my eyes. You've heard this rhyme before.

★

In came a fisherman, he wanted a bride, we held up a seal and gave him a stamp, then hit him with a sickle, let go a little spittle, threw him off a bridge, then peed on the wall. With a magical broom, the wind sang sweep, like an oar in air we ascend. We power the instrument and apply a salve, uncover the ghost behind *fig*. Mistake it for an omen then quiet the cloud, the cloud just there seen through a cataract. We wallow in shallow, stick to the surfeit, singularly tremble, are immune to sting. We consult the leaves and measure the air.

*

It was a simple mallet. It spoke simply, whammo, blam, I understood perfectly. Its oscillations filled the dark in waves of blue, some green and felt like no other mallet in my life. Its use was not significant only its shape, after all it was a tool.

*

Sunday, the silver of asphodel will not save me. If only I were rich. I could write 'happiness'.

*

If Monday a whole world begins, if to build a flower, if naked at the base of a sycamore, if animated camou-flaged bark, if a tear in front of a weather-swept lens, or if laughter at the banquet-crazy table, if eyes opening an ingenious fire, if only to paint this ray only.

*

I had been working the mine for scraps of dust. Head bent for years. When I came up the years had gone. The world was not the world and children were whizzing past me now, with blurred exuberance and CGI forcefulness. What to do as the boards rotted and gave. The paint peeled, macadam lumpy.

*

What is a man but a papered miscellany, a bio furnace blowing coal, a waste treatment plant manufacturing bluster, an open signal full of seawater, a dark stranger turning over the dark next to you.

*

Friday ends in a burning shack. A humpback oratorio spewing roses. The swashbuckler enters from the right singing his pantaloons off. The glint off his sword performs a vast speech, the torch inside an idea, pinwheel sparks squealing on the commons, simply exhaustion after a long day with small children. Hats airborne.

*

This body only lasts for so many days. It's got a shelf life. It's got time-lapse, time-based carbon life. There's you and it and now you are it. That's the paradigm. Dream and enter this evolutionary atmosphere, highly susceptible to laws of gravity, entropy, falling at a startling velocity. Flying is out or so significantly not the same as to be pretty much out.

*

It wasn't meant to be this way. Let me do this now. I don't want to do it again. Let it be said I made an attempt to give relief to the dark. It didn't work. Won't work. Don't really want it to work. It's hard to say. Old as the world itself, war toy and doll, born from necessity to do grown-up work. To slumber in a dark full of memory and figure, to yellow on shelves in catalogs, to become a fit subject for a poem. To be classified, mistakenly, for always.

*

Dreams are such a solid state and then porous and then heavy wet air evaporating, you know: the Blue Fairy walked the bridge-rail over concrete gardens, below her cars and cows packed tightly, sliding, screeching before awaking into the sparkling air of modern poetry.

*

And so the singer cast a shadow. It was like every other shadow and so we were comforted. The song was summer itself. Green and a special blue went into all of us. We sat and sweated in our chairs. It wasn't exactly pretty when the song, the green and blue, went into our heads.

*

In chairs we continue the odd alignment of earth in its bearings, the dirt inside bread, spinning and adjusting our breath. But enough of the singer and the special song of summer. We were tired of you, grew tired of these greens and blues, tired of the ray's long sad decline. It bent way down and didn't feel special anymore.

*

It wasn't meant to be this way, the wind leaning, the trees sway, the stars there. Take the long walk home past shadows, alleys, and culverts past streets in midnight past footsteps out there. Take the long walk take the verdigris the periwinkle above it the soot and sirens and odd laughter in the park. Take the promise and transform the man. Look hard into the air.

*

The shadow cast a singer. It was like every other shadow and so we were comforted. But who would stay the same even if the ray's report is the same. I am changing and you know about this too. The fuzz haloed with heat lines in a cartoon. I am summer the shadow the song and the solstice. Green and a special blue went into all of us.

Tiny Blast

Just a small song with a dash of spite.
A tiny thistle below the belt.

That's it, you know,
the twinge inside this fabulous cerulean.

Don't back away. Turtle into it
with your little force.

The steady one wins this enterprise.
This bingo shouter. This bridge of sighs.

And now that you're here be brave.
Be everyway alive.

Tradition & the Indivisible Talent

If all the world says something
we think then we know something
don't we? And then the blank screen
or memory again. You crazy.
No, you crazy. It's like this
but almost always
when time-lapsed words
and weather-swept flowering trees
move in empathetic wind.
I am rooted but alive.
I am flowering and dying.
I am you the wind says, the wind.

The embiggened afternoon
was just getting started
and to be adrift and stuck
can be a pleasant sensation
like loving abstraction
or a particular object's nimbus.
Pick one and look at it,
human or digital, vegetable,
mineral, alive or dying,
it's all atomic anyhow
much closer, the electron
part of being. Being,
it's a small word.
After all absence makes
the particles move faster.
The path tilted up to the right
and the angled view
so dramatic in boisterous sun.

When a thought's thingness
begins to move, to become
unmoored and you ride

the current with your head,
feel yourself lift off like
birdsong caught in the inner ear
even the curios seem animated
in their dusty shelves –
the song is alive.
That part of tradition.

Birdsong and daybreak,
are they not the same at the root?
Twigs torn from brambles
nest and house this cooing thing.
Close your eyes. The notes
imprint their solar magic homing
a musical refrain built out
in a sculptural vortex –
the applause of rushes
sung into a larger sequence.
The sky. And now the word is fire,
fire in the heart, fire in the head.
Fire above and fire in bed –
seemingly the only element
to get gilded up in song.

How about dirt? I love you
like dirt. I miss you dirty mouth,
dirty smile, oh, and my dirt
is your dirt is nice also.
Closer to the ground, perhaps,
on the ground, that's real enough
and those goddamn spuggies
are fledged and it's spring
and the books in my shelves
in my head have all turned. Nothing
but earth and peat and mold
and rich soft living manna
you can breathe. The must
at the root of it all, desire
and wanting, must know.

Lullaby

All animals like to nuzzle with their soft parts

what of it when you see the leafy conflagration in spring

a reminiscing eventual in small wistful bursts

the rhythm of sweeping

everything orbiting in this path

the daytime moon and the mourning dove

both are gray and still with us

even today what is soft and has depth is pleasant

Saturday can be like this too alone in the garage

the organic symphony encircling

the furrowed lanes of mint and clover

remember this and breathe deeply when you can

Wisdom is a kindly spirit but does it love me? And righteousness? There's nothing in it.

[1] To poetry I leave my senses, my deregulation, custodial duties, and to be a janitor is a great consolation.

[2] It gave me my mother back through all her years.

[3] To love these children, so full of neurons and consciousness. What joy to clean up and put a shine on their mess.

[4] To my mother I leave my veil, my wing, the window and time. I, artifact. In this age the hand is a voice.

[5] I leave the voice, the wonder, the mirror, and my lens, bent and beholden to the worm, leaf-work in wrought iron, eerie illuminations and deep-sea vision.

[6] I've seen the Eurostar, the drunken boat, and Davy Jones' Locker. I've seen Spanish galleons and the H.S. Mauberly covered in brine.

[7] There is this line from cloud dander to the solo bulb of mourning, a string through common prayer.

[8] I like it when the gray-green shadows suddenly dayglo over the rushes. The wind in my head.

[9] To write is an equal and opposite reaction my comrade, communard, my friendo.

[10] What is it finally thinking what in winter's dusty alcove, the body tocks. The day was cloudy. The light muddy, dreary when they took it down.

[11] To Times Roman I give my stammer, my sullenness, my new world violence, form and all that, forms, and all that paper, gusts. Little buttress.

[12] I send love and weapons to everyone possessed with night visions.

[13] When those green lights flash and blink, is that it? When the 'it' continues strangely for a bit, then falls into a line, is it over?

[14] I quantified daily the wonder in the grain.

[15] I found I was over and singular yet many, the

many and the singular, the many and the evolutionary, the many in the grain. Many more.

[16] Who in hell am I writing for?

[17] This vision is silly, teenage, and mine, a spot on the negative, a hole in composition. I quantify, I loaf, I wonder, I find, I rev.

[18] Here the days' mud, night is a satellite, and anger, my cleft, my birthmark and star.

[19] Anger might be a better way to say 'I love you', truer than 'how are you in space'? Are you cold, can I get you a blanket?

[20] To the polestar I leave my alien regalia, my off-world headdress. I leave acoustic forms in time, blooming, sudsy, inconsolable.

[21] If you are unsatisfied, then welcome.

[22] Here there are people working every corner of every inch of grass. The meticulously arranged outside reminds me of ocean and feels old.

[23] In space the letterforms 'I love' oscillate in waves.

[24] I lose myself in waves speaking the half of me that forgot to say 'goodbye' when I meant to say 'how come'.

[25] Memory continues to bloom. More songs about death and dying, songs of inexperience.

[26] More songs about being and loss, being in loss, more songs about seeing and feeling.

[27] If you are critical, all the better to see and to miss it, to misunderstand, to fail at empathy and love, to not understand love and to love, to be diseverything and to love, whatever.

[28] To mercy I leave whatever.

True Discourse on Power

When I say the ghost has begun
you understand what is being said.
That time is not how we keep it
    or measure
first there was then wasn't...
It twitters and swerves like
    the evening news.
Now outside is 3D. Inside non-
    representational space.
Every law has an outside
    and inside
I have witnessed cruelty
break and gulp and sweat then
    punch out a smile.
To be awake. This talking in space.
To be absorbed in the ongoing.
Belief's a shadow to be looked into
    and into
until relief is gone. The dark
triangle settled in the midst of
    traffic is on us.
Time comes in adverbial bursts,
a glass of beer, a smoke ...
The evening air refreshes, startles,
and the questions grow deeper like
    shadows across storefronts.
A forsythia ticking against
    the dirty pane.
This was time. Up. Down. Up.
And you were a part of it.
If I say it can you feel it now?
Imagine. Lightning strikes. Rain
    falls and drives.
Clouds pass. Night clarified. Stars.

In silent pictures the tree falls
     in the optic nerve.
The sound is chemistry.
There's no getting to it or if
     getting to it
feels like the actual sound
     is that silence?
Alone here with my shadows
     drawn ...
So what's this about?
A horse and a castle, a tree
     and its leaving?
What's this about in solitary
     splendor?
The undertow and its threshold,
a door and the opening sky?
Or because a play of reflection
     lit up my bumper
and caught my eyes
I saw the shadow of a falcon.
Because a sound a poor man
     uttered
reached my ear I fell into song.
If the syntax of loyalty is not tragic
     then what is the wager?
If there were time, would it be ours?

A Note on the Text

The good poets defy things
with their heart

This is how a fragment
enters the people

Don't say beauty say the beautiful
say the people

Say it is through chants that writing
entered the people

Their imagery and love of nature,
englutted flowers

This place of fleshlessness
Here is my song

the only recourse of sun
Even its smallest syllables

can be sown into the mouth
It is on the tongue the sun abides

Two syllables fastened
to each end

To stretch the vocal pattern
Its linenlike thread

Oversong

Tonight I am down to my soul
Jason Molina

To be dark, to darken
to obscure, shade, dim

to tone down, to lower
overshadow, eclipse

to obfuscate, adumbrate
to cast into the shade

becloud, bedim, be-
darken, to cast a shadow

throw a shade, throw
a shadow, to doubt

to dusk, extinguish
to put out, blow out

to exit, veil, shroud
to murk, cloud, to jet

in darkness, Vesta
midnight, Hypnos

Thanatos, dead of night
sunless, dusky, pitch

starless, swart, tenebrous
inky, Erebus, Orpheus

vestral, twilit, sooty, blae…

Bardo

I've spent my life
in a lone mechanical whine,

this combustion far off.

How fathomless to be
embedded in glacial ice,

what piece of self hiding there.

I am not sure about meaning
but understand the wave.

No more Novalis out loud.

No Juan de la Cruz singing
'I do not die to die'.

No solstice, midhaven, *midi,* nor twilight.

No 'isn't it amazing', no
none of that.

To crow, to crown, to cry, to crumble.

The trees the air warms into
a bright something

a bluish nothing into

clicks and pops
bursts and percussive runs.

I come with my asymmetries,
my untutored imagination.

Heathenish,

my homespun vision
sponsored by the winter sky.

Then someone said nether,
someone whirr.

And if I say the words
will you know them?

Is there world?
Are they still calling it that?

Archeophonics

I'm just visiting this voice
I'm just visiting the molecular structures
    that say what I am saying
I am just visiting the world at this moment
    and it's on fire
It's always been on fire

I'm saying this and it's saying me
That's how it works, seesaw like
The archive in the mouth and the archive is on fire
That's the story
The sun and the body and the body in the sun

It was like this just like this
The world that's coming toward me
And the world around me
Around me are words saying this
    saying fire
Saying something or all of it

Field Recordings

For today's tourist, orientation is impossible
                    Arthur Rimbaud

I. LANGUOR

The old language
is the old language,
with its lance and greaves,
broken shields
and hammered vowels;
a stairway ascending
into a mirror – see it
climb the old helix,
beneath a scarred
and chipped northerly sky,
rotunda blue.

Sing genetic cloud forms
mirroring the syntax
in reflection, and what
would you have?

Paving stones, rhetoric,
the coping of bridges,
leanings, what
is taken from *res*?
To reconstruct? To re-
cognize the categories
have failed? That
the index was a lyre.

The lists have grown
lonely, far from home,
houses of worship,
roofs, toy stores and

liquor stores, names,
historical furniture,
descriptions of architecture,
patina in a fanfare city.

I have eaten the air
of that city.

The old language
says the apple
is the old apple,
it spoke
in categories
and gave her all
the dance floor
she needed, all
those vocab-
ularies and animal
nights before her,
we see through
to spotted fur.

Lithe, the taut
syllables in apple
and the ecstasy of
naming. Or was it
knowing? Windows
swing open.
The chest
a hammering thing.

This hammering
thing, life as I've
known it, know me,
is over. I might as well
say it. The apples lie
scattered on ground.

The earth reclaims
its booty right be-
fore the eyes. So
swiftly the letters
replace, the
letters dearrange

and uncompose
the self in itself.
The orchestral side
is taking away me.

These letters
no longer anchor.

The world today
is slowcore,
a rhythm section
dragging.

At the moment
I drag and solo
in a bitten landscape,
torn vowels
that sound out vowel
or sadness like glitter
sprinkled in a mind.

A sun-slashed parking lot,
thinking a poem
stalled
in the broken
surround.

See the chubby kid dazed,
his spilled bike,
more debris,
CVS in the distance.

Remember me
to convenience stores.
I saw this too
every life of my day
yet I ate, I had money,
and a car.

There were markets
used bookstores
trellises and brick.

These were the words
I could see
thinking of the body.

It's strange here
all the names in me.
The gain and its foliage.

In my last rotation
it was hard to tune in.
The dial was faulty.

The static lovely.
It spoke to me
through a grubby transom.

Was that a cathedral bell
or the air conditioner?
Crisp air coming in.

Looking out the frame
I studied grass.
So many pages blank.

It's hard to look that close.
I watched from a high window
while I slept.

Faces fly by
in random litter,
as September rays
hit the lawns.
The high-lit
dry white shafts
slightly vintaging.
The bright
horizon preening
in fife air.

The days go and
are gone.
The night's gone
before us,
a neon cursive glow.
If only to dream
awhile, through
an ascending scale
of history, its ill be-
gotten schemes,
statecraft, unwieldy
theatrical devices.

The old language
renews the pundits'
chatter, can sometimes
bunch in groups,
power jumbotrons,
or one's laughter
in particular.
Just now, out
the car window
paper flags
and ballots kite.

Feel the parade
air on your skin.
A cotton shirt
touching it. The
manufactured rays
are ancient, fall
through a time-gone
ticker tape array.
The floats and whorls
and banners above.

The old language
dozing in sun.

6. STRANGENESS BECOMES YOU

The old language is
the old language.
It don't mean shit.

It's not where you begin
it's how you finish.
Everyone's got beer muscles
when they're young.

Try as you must.
Break as you will.
Solo in space
clinging to space.

Fuck, the air said
passing a corner,
a long ropy snot
hitting a gutter.

To know something
and fail.
Why discount it?
The onslaught of eyes
beneath a fuck-you sky.

The syntax breaks down
its mangled draft and says,
one day the poor
will have nothing
to eat but the rich.

I hate that, when syntax
connects me to the rich.

I hate how syntax
connects me to shit,
or say the day
is jeweled and burning,
the fires banking,
and none of its letters
produce the horror
at the heart of the index.
The old document
hangs over the twinned
stair of murder
and something else –
that original slap of glove.

The project is archival,
all that blood in the mouth.
The old language
could have told you,
it's too late,
we watched you die,
watched you move
through shocking losses
and the solo flight
you are taking back
into the old language.

It's the same but different,
different now.
The mouth knows the bit,
the taste of it.

It's strange here, all this time in me and time around me. I was trying to climb out from under 5AM thinking outside the truck and its engine are real.

Today the slinky is 70 years old. Next year my body will be 57: it was human, it was American, it was a piece of big data, it was employed, it loved and mourned the documents behind a people.

In my time I loved people.

9. RIME

It was a language to eat the sky
a language to say goodbye

standing with others
standing in the dust.

The old language
continues its dialogues

in ordinary dust.

When Orbital Proximity Feels Creepy

Right now there are teenage microwaves
screaming through your body
while you are having text with me.
This is the moment I'll need you to sing
    with me.
I am making my way in some dark room
looking for other structures to love.
From the left something speaking
    I can't identify.
The floor goes unfixed and moving
and this doesn't happen only at night
but during the day when I don't want
    to think on it.
That I saw a blood-orange ball caught
    out my window.
That I'm listening to light and it said time.
I'm listening to time, it says, ha.
You need to be howling at bloody torn space.
Need to be spooked out of your hidey-hole
    and its glowing mess.
But I love this ball I'm riding on.
The strange hunk of metal and rock whizzing
    around my loves and my loving.
The fact I spin and it spins and everything
    is spinning close up.
From far away it's so cool.
I guess they call this physics or they call it laws.
If they're so well-made, why do we suffer?
I thought the day was opening
but now I see it's already gone.
Outside the cruel dove has a broken window.
The day isn't friendly.
Who are you to me?
A way to understand the floor?

The floor that holds me up and leaves me
        standing.
I don't know where to go.
Me, Tuesday at 5 p.m.
What does it mean to be in a room,
        any room.
The wind banging against the clapboard.
I know enough to see the cracked pane
isn't going to be fixed anytime soon.
Who has time for such things in the song?
Breaking. Blooming.
The wobble of light on wood-grain late
        in the day.
In the loneliness of orange.
In the loveliness of orange.

Release the Darkness to New Lichen

But I found a way to say no
to the wood in my house

it kept creaking
wouldn't stop talking

I found a way to say no

I need to be standing
in the warmth of the wood
that the sun made

I need to find myself dissolving

otherwise it is all otherwise
I'm lost, did I say that

I saw the frill of light today
walking on the path

could you hear the stirring
in the wood, pine needles
and the branches

was it wind or a creature
am I here or is it over

this was the first day
the nothing day
in the nothing year

it gave me courage

it gave hints of blue,
clouds, electrical
and dancing

it gave me rays
I've never seen

shooting down
touching things

this was the first day

This World Is Not Conclusion

for and after Emily Dickinson

When I look out your window I see another window
I see a wedding in my brain, a stylus and a groove
a voice waving there

When I look out your window I see another window
these trees are not real they grow out of air
they fell like dust they fell

So singing is seeing and vision is music
I saw diadems and crowns, daisies and bees, ribbons, robins,
    and disks of snow
sprung effects in pencil-light

When I look out your window I see another window
I see a fire and a girl, crimson hair and hazel eyes
a public in the sky

When the world comes back it will be recorded sound
that cooing shrub will be known as dickinson
the syllabic, fricative, percussive, and phatic will tear open

Out your window I see another window
I see a funeral in the air I see alabaster space
I read circumference there

Song

I want color to braid,
to bleed, want song
to fly to flex to think
in lines. To work
the pulp, to open up
this cardinal feeling
in green.

The hardest part
is the songbirds
and their fugue state,
fug state, fuck it.
The world is neon
in the gloaming quiet.

I am willing to walk
away, willing to be
on fire, to blaze
to Blake, to sink
into the moon's
aphorism and
its garden of figures.

The moon above
my life. It's rough
and real tonight,
cold fusion
reflecting sun.
There is a quaver,
a gibbous light
to this equation.

Puzzling rays full
of dinghies, pixies,
kobolds, and gems,

heroes, songsters,
and your face.
The strangeness
becomes you,
darling night.

Pretty Sweety

Here there are small animals
foraging and content

Perhaps this is what's called
perhaps love is a small animal foraging

content entirely with its mouth there
with the ant and the sun and fur

This is a strange view
sunlight and furlight and a mouth

busy with nature
a mouth busy with its bloom

a mouth blooming loveliness

Rainy Days and Mondays

Over the all this and
under the all that

between this yes
and that yes

hauntedness

between the girl
and arrows

the long ago
and far away

between galaxy
and litter

talking to myself
for now

a song

Sentences in a Synapse Field

For I wanted sound / to
dig into sound

For snow and blood / for
wine and mirrors / for
electrons / and electricity

For debris / for damaged art / our
collective fortune / future

For as long as there have been soldiers / there
have been poets / for as long as poets
there has been a bridge

For I wanted to hold a room in silence
For debris flooding back into a wave

For as long as particles / a charge / for
it should be incredulity / to be alive

For these things that can be told / until
mystery becomes elegy

For it was March going into April / for
the day was / speaking the day

For what you thought / for
what you buried / for
who you are /

How to Read

for Rosmarie Waldrop

A world of light and a world of openism

A syntax of heat and dynamism

A human world mewling in the dark

A giganto space of silence, time

A mind on fire in the heat of the quest

Rhythm percussion assonance

Energetic silent magic

A textual nimbus, air born

A Winding Sheet for Summer

1.

I wanted out of the past so I ate the air,
    it took me further into air.
It cut me, an iridescent chord
    of geometric light.
I breathed deep, it lit me up, it was good.
All these years, lightning, rain, the sky,
    its little daisies.
Memento mori and lux.

2.

And you can't blame me.
This daisy-feeling.
I was a poet with a death-style of my own
    waking.
I occupy the rest of it.
A blue-green leaving feeling.
To no longer belong to a body sometimes
    open to air.
In rain, in early morning rain.

3.

Today was the day of the amphitheater in mind.
The day of a dreaming speech where the light is dope
    and that's all you can say.
When a feeling degrades and evolves into thought like
    2AM dilated, revealed a star.
It will say this long agony is great being awake.
It is being lovely now.

4.

All the stars are here that belonged to whatever
    was speaking.
I built my life out of what was left of me.
Sky and its procedures.
A romanticism of clouds, trees, pale crenellations,
    and poetry.
A musical joybang.
Touching everything.

5.

When the words come back their fictions remain.
Thunderheads and rain, lexical waters raking gutters,
    carving a world.
The stylus will live in the flash.
A daring light from pewter to whatever.
Now discrete observations produce undramatic sound,
    like I am a bubble,
make me the sea. O, make me the sea.

6.

For a long time the names of things and things unnamed.
For a long time hawks and their chicks, fox and their cubs,
    mice and their mice.
For a long time bunnies and boojum, and a name
    for every bird in me.
I am native to feathers – their netherside.

7.

The sun was a goldish wave taped to a book.
A wavy diagram in a fusty book.
Foxed old wave.
A soft electro-fuzz enters the head.
A soft fuzzy opiate lightness.
What could be the message in this
    pointillist masquerade.
What use memory.

8.

I came from a different world.
I will die in it.
Someone saw it, I love them for seeing it.
I love seeing it with them.
Love watching it die in me.
It wasn't behind or beside me.
Finding it wasn't it.
Being it was everything.
That was the thing I thought as I fell.

9.

I am that thing in morning, whatever motors in the skull,
    something is claimed.
Sudden rain keeps it real.
Rooftops from the window look stunned.
    Cleansed.
Looking out over the day, the pale performing day.
I always consult the air before composing air.

10.

And what have you been given, the blue nothing asks,
    who are you under clanging brass?
Who are you, Saturday; sing to me.
See the crows thread summerismus.
Afternoon shade mirrors an issuelessness.
A perfection of beetle slowly treading summer's blade.
The leaves broadcast color.
I was born in summer, my conqueror,
    breaking into wisteria.

11.

The sun was a golden rag nailed to a ladder.
And here the marigolds grow down to the banks.
The mayflies drowse above water.
How then the dazzling surface and its dictions
    under piled clouds,
and clouds sitting there by place and sound.
One thing. This thing and sound glitters.
Indicative transitive particular battles the void.
All afternoon a green-gold silent light
    on the spotted grass, sprung.

12.

I know it's summer even if I can't decipher the call.
I believe in the birds haunting me. I held on.
I'm full of bluster but also full of vision.
I'm not ready to put the book down.
To stop singing bright spots thrilling the quicksilver
    over my torrent.
I make sounds, forget to die. I call it living,
    this inhuman conch in the ear.
A pewter sensation and wind.

13.

The sun remains a yellow sail tacked to the sky.
I am climbing air here. I am here
      in the open.
The kestrel swerves.
Its silent kerning.
A stunning calibration of nothing.
I'm left to see.

Bewitched

When I look
to the east
I could not
find you
in the west
where the light
was dying you
were not there
northerly the sky
grew pitch
silence to the south
there was
only billowing

Now to go over
to greet
the small wind
as the huge
blows by
horn blind
and feathered
what is this
former swaying
this deep pomp
beyond and
waiting
crouched and
magnified

Is the word
a cunning bird
even in new
dark I will not
be quiet, the
feathering
covering me

I will not turn
away showing
my face and
love the words
pouring from
your mouth

Po-lyph-o-ny it was
a music to me
a freaky effluvium
entering me lit
with that speak
with its thick
embryonic music
born into a strange
new light darker
than any like
I had known
before, polyphony
spoke to me

It was a
language
to eat the sky
a language
to say goodbye
standing
with others
standing in
the dust
the old language
continues its
dialogues in
ordinary dust

Now the sun was
a bower of
rusty cables

its deep center
flashing, welding
this room
to silence
an ascension
hard and hauling
heaves above
the time and
its tether

When I think
all you have
done I
think on all
of this and you
know the way
I trod the path
dissembled
with leaves
under the ghosting
shades an elm made
and discovered
the pages of
my book
open to greet me

In the poem
I am thick
with dream
my limbs heavy
forcing myself
to wake into
striated dusks
rising through
the stratum
a question
in my brain

Index of Poem Titles